WHAT HAPPENED NEXT?

GREAT
EVENTS

Richard Tames

FRANKLIN WATTS

NEW YORK • CHICAGO • LONDON • TORONTO • SYDNEY

© 1995 Franklin Watts

Franklin Watts
95 Madison Avenue
New York, NY 10016

Library of Congress Cataloging-in-Publication Data
Tames, Richard
     Great events / by Richard Tames
        p. cm.—(What happened next?)
     Includes index.
     ISBN 0-531-14358-9 (lib. bdg.)
     1. History, Modern—Juvenile literature. 2. Military history,
Modern—Juvenile literature. [1. History, Modern. 2. Military
history. Modern.] I. Title II. Series.
     D208.T36 1995   94-31354
     909.82—dc20   CIP AC

10 9 8 7 6 5 4 3 2 1

A CIP catalogue record for this book is available from the British Library.

Series editor: Belinda Weber
Designer: Edward Kinsey
Illustrators: Ruth Levy
Picture researcher: Diana Morris

Photographs: AKG, London: 5t (Guildhall Art Gallery, London), 6b, 10t (Yale University Art Gallery, New Haven),
10bl (photo Brich Lessing), 11tl (Hofburg, Vienna), 11tr (Musée Versailles), 16t (Musée Versailles), 16b, 18br
(Musée Versailles), 23t, 24b, 25b, 28c,34t. Ancient Art & Architecture Collection: 21b. Bridgeman Art Library: cover l
(Musée Carnavalet, Paris) 18bl (Aspley House, London), 21t (Royal Library, Stockholm), 22t (Musée Marmottan,
Paris), 22bl (Forbes Magazine Collection, New York), 28c (S.J. Phillips, London), 28b (Private Collection). Jean
Loup-Charmet: 13t. e.t. archive: 7t (Musée Versailles), 9t, 12c, 18t, (Musée Versailles), 19t (Musée d'Orsay, Paris),
19c, 28t, 36b, 37tr, 40bl, 40br (National Archives, Washington). Mary Evans Picture Library: 6l, 9b, 10br, 12b, 20t,
20b, 22br, 24-5t, 26t, 30c, 31t, 32b, 33t (Alexander Melledin Collection). Giraudon/Bridgeman Art Library: 13b
(Musée Carnavalet, Paris), 15b (Musée Versailles). Robert Harding Picture Library: 12t. Hulton Deutsch: 28br, 30t,
31bl, 32t, 33b, 38b. Lauros/Giraudon/Bridgman Art Library: 17t (Chateau de Malmaison, Paris). Peter Newark's
Pictures: 5b, 8b, 14t, 15t. Popperfoto: 26b, 27b, 28b, 29t, 31br, 34bl, 34br, 35t, 35b, 36t, 37tl, 37b, 38b, 39t, 39b, 40t.

Printed in Belgium.

CONTENTS

One of the most important things to learn about the past is that great events might not have turned out the way that they actually did. History is cluttered with riots that never became revolutions and brilliant ideas that were never turned into inventions that really worked. History is just as much the story of what might have been as it is the story of what was.

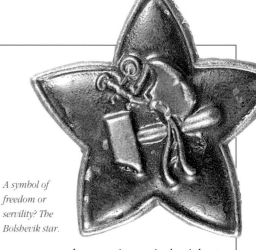

A symbol of freedom or servility? The Bolshevik star.

This book is about six great turning points in history. Each one of them began a chain of events that became a matter of life or death for millions of people. Each might have turned out quite differently.

THE PAST WE NEVER HAD

JUST SUPPOSE...

During the crisis leading up to America's fight for its independence, many people on both sides wanted to try to find a peaceful solution to the quarrel between the American colonists and the British Crown. One suggestion was that the capital of the British empire should be moved from London to Philadelphia, which was the biggest colonial city at that time.

It wasn't such a poorly thought out idea. The population of the American colonies was growing fast. With so much unsettled land to expand into, the area might soon be larger than Britain itself. To the north, an immense new country - the future Canada - had just

A symbol of military tradition – a Samauri sword from Japan.

been conquered for the Crown only a few years before. To the south were the rich plantations of the West Indies, probably the most valuable of all British possessions. Between them these lands really did represent a "New World."

LIVING IN GEORGELAND?

If George III had gone to live in North America perhaps this would have kept the colonies loyal. Perhaps all the English-speaking colonies of the area, including the West Indies, could have become a single country - "United Georgeland," ruled from "New London."

But if that had happened, Britain itself might have felt cut off or oppressed by a distant government, in which its people played no part - leading Britain to rise in revolt, rather that the other way around.

BRITISH-STYLE RULE?

When the French revolution broke out many British people welcomed it because it began with the calling of the Estates General - the French parliament - for the first time for more than a century. Perhaps this would mean the French would get a British-style government, in which Parliament and the king worked together.

However, the British statesman and writer Edmund Burke warned that events in France would

The French king had a well-trained army. But would they fight against their fellow Frenchmen?

become increasingly violent. And that is just what happened, until an ambitious general ended the chaos by seizing power and making himself a dictator. But what if Napoleon had been killed while he was a junior officer fighting in the front line to make a name for himself? Would another general have seized power anyway? Or might revolutionary France have collapsed into civil war?

We will never know the answers to these questions. But we do know that some events have a huge impact on history - changing the lives of millions of people. And this book looks at six such events, asking *what happened next?*

IS THIS THE END OF THE REBELLION?

King George III was a powerful force in politics. He ruled England and her colonies from 1760-1820.

The armed rebellion in Britain's American colonies has been going on for thirty months. How much longer can it continue? And what can be done to stop it?

THE BRITISH POINT OF VIEW

Britain's conquest of Canada means that American colonists are no longer threatened by the French and their Indian allies. American safety has been bought with British blood and British taxes. It is only fair that Americans should contribute to the upkeep of the troops who continue to protect them.

In 1763 the British government asked agents of the colonies in London how each colony might raise money to pay for the army that guards them. They offered no suggestions.

In 1765 the government passed a Stamp Act that would have raised cash by taxing legal documents and such luxuries as newspapers, cards, and dice. This is an entirely normal tax in Britain and would have raised enough to pay only a third of the total cost of American defense. What happened? Protests, riots, and even attacks on His Majesty's officials! Ever since then, Britain has been trying to get Americans to pay their fair share.

Americans anger the king in many other ways. They evade taxes on trade by smuggling. They damage trade by refusing to buy British goods. And they defy the Proclamation Line, which sets a western boundary of settlement and safeguards the hunting grounds of the Indian tribes.

THE AMERICAN POINT OF VIEW

The British government has no right to impose taxes on the American colonies because the colonies elect no members of Parliament and therefore lack representatives to give their point of view and give consent on their behalf.

It is unjust to say that Americans make no effort in their own defense. Almost every able-bodied man has to serve in the militia. So Americans prove their willingness to defend their land against His Majesty's enemies with their lives – not just by the payment of a few pennies in taxes!

The colonists have tried to defend their interests by sound reason and peaceful argument. But the British government has responded with laws that oppose the very freedoms that are the birthright of all who are born of British stock – whether they make their home in the Old World or in the New!

The Proclamation Line marked the western boundary of settlement. It was defended by the British.

Proclamation Line

Indian Reserve

Colonies

Atlantic Ocean

Able-bodied Americans served in the militia.

WHO STARTED

In September 1774 leaders of twelve of the thirteen colonies met in Philadelphia as a "Continental Congress". They condemned British interference and confirmed the right of each colony to pass its own laws and raise its own taxes. In February 1775 Parliament declared Massachusetts to be in a state of rebellion. British troops and ships had a secure hold on its capital, Boston, but weapons to arm a force of 15,000 colonists were being stockpiled at Concord, only 16 miles (26 km) away. In April, British troops were sent from Boston to seize the armory.

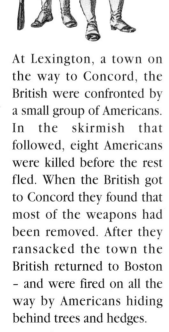

British soldiers fought on behalf of their king, defending the colonies from attack.

DO THEY REALLY WANT INDEPENDENCE?

At Lexington, a town on the way to Concord, the British were confronted by a small group of Americans. In the skirmish that followed, eight Americans were killed before the rest fled. When the British got to Concord they found that most of the weapons had been removed. After they ransacked the town the British returned to Boston - and were fired on all the way by Americans hiding behind trees and hedges.

A second Continental Congress was held in May 1775. It decided to form a Continental Army and appointed a Virginia slave owner as its commander - a man called George Washington. Despite this warlike move, the Congress also renewed its efforts to find a peaceful solution to the crisis and sent a petition to King George III calling for reconciliation. It was never presented because it was known that the king would be unwilling to receive it.

In the autumn of 1775 an American invasion of Canada began well but ended in disaster at Quebec. A siege of Boston proved more successful, and from March 7 to 17, 1776, the British evacuated their garrison and more than 1,000 Loyalists who refused to join the rebellion. It is said that many more supported the uprising only out of fear of being tarred and feathered by so-called Sons of Liberty.

On July 4, 1776, the Continental Congress approved a formal "Declaration of Independence."

The Sons of Liberty's justice was swift and humiliating. Loyalists were drenched with tar and then coated with feathers.

Rebel forces are fighting under a flag of 13 red and white stripes - with a Union Jack in the corner! Surely this shows how confused loyalties are in this unhappy country!

WHO IS WINNING THE WAR?

In August 1776 the British inflicted a major defeat on the rebels at a battle fought on Long Island, near New York. The British lost fewer than 400 men, but about 1,500 Americans were killed or captured - including two

THE SHOOTING?

George Washington was appointed commander in chief of the Continental Army in 1775.

The sites of the major battles. The Continental Army could only rely on a few thousand regular troops and often fought with the help of volunteer militia.

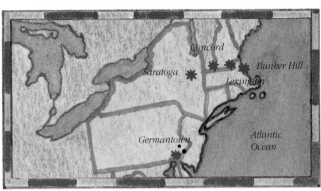

generals. In September, British troops occupied New York, and in October they defeated the retreating American army two more times.

RETREAT ACROSS THE DELAWARE

Also in October a makeshift American naval force was routed on Lake Champlain. In December British forces occupied Rhode Island. General Washington was forced to retreat across the Delaware River from New Jersey into Pennsylvania.

THE TABLES ARE TURNED

On December 26, 1776, Washington turned the tables on his pursuers and led 2,400 rebel troops in a daring crossing of the

Delaware River to take 1,600 German mercenaries entirely by surprise - 106 were killed and 918 taken prisoner. A week later, at Princeton, Washington again shocked his enemy with a surprise attack. In April 1777 the Americans were further heartened by the arrival of the first volunteer troops from Britain's traditional enemy, France.

AND TURNED AGAIN

During the summer of 1777 the British launched two main offensives. Under the command of General John Burgoyne, troops advanced from Canada to take Albany, the capital of New York Colony. This first offensive drove a wedge between the colonies of New England and the other American colonies.

The second offensive, commanded by General William Howe, saw troops marching on Philadelphia, the largest city in the colonies. At Brandywine Creek, on September 11, Howe outmaneuvered Washington, forcing him to pull back from what should have been a good defensive position. The Americans

Washington and his troops crossed the Delaware River in December 1776 to surprise a group of German mercenaries.

lost 1,000 men, but the British, although on the attack, lost fewer than 600 and went on to occupy Philadelphia. On October 4, Washington was defeated yet again at Germantown. His troops became confused in thick fog and fired on each other. Altogether, the rebels lost about 700 men.

SURRENDER AT SARATOGA

After these disasters it must have cheered the rebels to learn that on October 17, General Burgoyne, surrounded by American forces that outnumbered him by more than three to one, surrendered his army

at Saratoga to the American commanding officer, General Horatio Gates. But the victory was not that dramatic. Fearing that the British would soon send reinforcements against him, Gates agreed to allow Burgoyne's approximately 5,000 captured soldiers to sail for England on condition that the men would not return to America to fight again.

A third winter of war approaches. The British are safe and snug in Philadelphia. But General Washington's twice beaten army face a hard time of it in the field. *Will the bitterly cold winter force General Washington to retreat?*

that had proved its superiority on three continents. And if Washington's men were in low spirits, perhaps they would want a new commander to lead them. Would they try to replace the Virginian with another leader? And if so, whom would they choose?

Washington's men had been beaten more often than they won. Perhaps the other officers were planning to take command? Did they replace him as commander?

WHAT HAPPENED NEXT?

DID WASHINGTON'S MEN DESERT?

The rebel armies had problems with desertion from the start. Their forces were made up of two main types of soldier. There were the regular troops of the Continental Army. Washington was trying to turn these soldiers into a disciplined force, capable of standing up to British regulars in a pitched battle. Then there were much larger numbers of colonial militia, who were badly equipped and poorly trained and therefore liable to panic or become confused in combat. In addition, there were also various freelance units who seemed willing to fight only when the mood took them. Every winter the rebel armies seemed to melt away. Would they return to the colors next spring for yet another campaign?

The rebel army soldiers were poorly trained and likely to desert.

COULD HE KEEP HIS MEN HEALTHY?

Washington had taken the precaution of having his men inoculated against smallpox. But to keep thousands of men healthy through an entire winter would require adequate supplies of tents, uniforms, and food. All the Continental Congress had to pay for these supplies was paper money, which many merchants thought was worthless and refused to accept. And even if supplies could be found and paid for, the British were sending out cavalry patrols in force to intercept convoys of supply wagons.

DID THE BRITISH TRY TO FINISH THE WAR QUICKLY?

T he British had the winter to rest, reorganize, and bring over reinforcements. If Washington's army had to survive a winter outdoors it would certainly be weakened and in low spirits when the campaigning started again in the spring. One full-scale battle was sure to smash it and prove once and for all that a mob of part-time amateurs could never beat a professional army of regulars,

Washington had been beaten twice as often as he had won.

Would he be replaced as commander?

His most recent defeats suggested that the more troops he was given to command, the less capable he was of controlling them.

HOW WOULD WASHINGTON

AND HIS MEN SURVIVE?

The winter weather was bitterly cold. Would Washington be able to keep his troops healthy enough to fight?

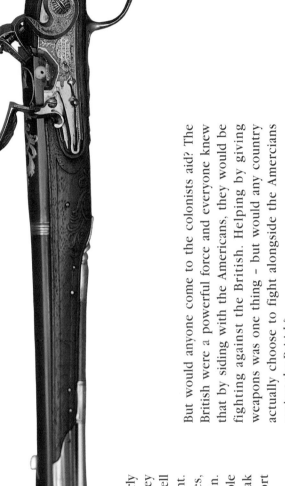

The American troops fought with foreign weapons, such as this French flintlock.

But would anyone come to the colonists aid? The British were a powerful force and everyone knew that by siding with the Americans, they would be fighting against the British. Helping by giving weapons was one thing - but would any country actually choose to fight alongside the Americans against the British?

DID ANYONE HELP THE AMERICANS?

T he Americans were outnumbered and poorly trained in comparison to the British. But they received help from French volunteers as well as cash and weapons from the French government. Adventurers from other European nations – Poles, Prussians, Dutchmen, and Swiss – also trickled in. Some were trained mercenaries who had valuable military experience. Some couldn't even speak English. Without really powerful outside support could the rebels ever hope to defeat the British?

WHAT REALLY HAPPENED IN THE WAR OF INDEPENDENCE?

The leaders of the American Revolution met on July 4, 1776, in Philadephia.

Congress had prepared a stockpile of flour, horseshoes, tools, and other provisions at Valley Forge, about 20 miles (32 km) from Philadelphia, to see the rebel forces through the winter. Unfortunately, the British discovered and removed these supplies before Washington could get hold of them.

Washington did not dare house his men in the towns of York or Lancaster where they would be vulnerable to surprise attack and encirclement. He felt much safer in Valley Forge, where small hills gave his troops a defensible position and local roads made it possible to bring in food from the surrounding area.

COLD AND HUNGRY

Washington's men suffered badly from cold, hunger, and disease. Many had to sleep out in the open, without even tents or makeshift shelters. Half had no blankets. A third had no shoes. Meat supplies ran

In the Declaration of Independence 13 colonies claimed independence from Great Britain.

out entirely by February. By the end of the winter Washington had lost about 2,000 men to exposure, disease and starvation.

From February onward, Washington's remaining men were reorganized and drilled by Baron von Steuben, a Prussian volunteer. The German didn't speak a word of English and had been retired for 14 years. In February, too, the rebels' hopes were renewed when France signed a formal treaty of alliance with Congress.

The British government later criticized General Howe for failing to move against Washington's demoralized troops in Valley Forge. General Howe resigned in 1778. In the same year British attempts at reconciliation were rejected by an adamant Congress, and Spain and the Netherlands also declared war on Britain.

1780

The rebels suffered a bad defeat in South Carolina, when 5,000 American prisoners were taken for a mere 260 British casualties. At Camden, also in South Carolina, the British routed a much larger force of rebels. In North Carolina, however, British regulars and Loyalist volunteers met a major defeat at King's Mountain.

1781

The British army was surrounded at the Battle of Cowpens, South Carolina; the Americans lost only 12 dead and 600 wounded. At Guildford Courthouse, North Carolina, the British defeated a much larger rebel force but lost almost half their own numbers. A similar success at Eutaw Springs, South Carolina, also cost the British dearly. In October, 1781, the Americans and their French allies finally won the decisive victory of the war at Yorktown, Virginia, bombarding the British army into submission with mortars and artillery.

Peace was finally concluded in 1783. Some 100,000 Loyalists left the newly independent United States. Most settled across the border in Canada or in Europe. General George Washington retired from the army in 1783. In 1789 he was elected first president of the United States.

George Washington was president of the new federal government of the United States from 1789 until his retirement in 1797.

DOES THIS MEAN CIVIL WAR IN FRANCE?

Who rules France? Is the most powerful and populous nation in Europe on the brink of civil war? Even the king accepts the need for reform – but events have been moving so fast that no one seems to be in control anymore.

THIS DIVIDED KINGDOM

France is a rich country – with millions of poor people. The royal palace at Versailles is the biggest in the world. The royal family lives in luxury, quite cut off from the ordinary people. King Louis XVI is kindly, shy, stubborn and not very clever. The queen, Austrian-born Marie-Antoinette, is beautiful, extravagant, and very unpopular. Aristocrats control all the top jobs in government, the army, and the law, but they pay no taxes! And the clergy pay taxes only when they want to. The middle classes - the merchants, lawyers and owners of small businesses – have been shut out from power despite the fact that they produce the wealth that others spend. The peasants - 80% of the population - are bowed down by taxes. Many have left the land for towns,

King Louis XVI was a kindly man, but his good intentions were neutralized by his lack of energy and of firmness.

Marie Antoinette married Louis XVI when she was just 15 years old. She was not popular in the French Court.

where they cannot find work and must beg in order to avoid starvation.

THE AMERICAN ADVENTURE

The French government has run out of money. That is what this great political crisis really amounts to. And the reason why there is no money left? Because of royal extravagance and foreign wars. France aided =50the rebels in the American colonies to attack its old enemy, Britain. The Americans got their freedom – but France has had to foot the bill!

Criticizing govern-ment policies has been a national sport among French writers and thinkers for half a century. Now even soldiers are doing it! Thousands of Frenchmen fought in America for the liberty of Americans. Many of them are starting to ask why there is so little liberty in France. The Americans have proclaimed that all men are equal. That may be true in America - but not in France where those who can afford it pay no taxes, and those who can't, do!

TIME FOR A CHANGE

In 1786 the king's controller-general of finance proposed the complete reform of the French tax system. The king and his ministers realized that this would mean ending the tax privileges of the nobles and clergy. Such a major change would need to be discussed. This meant summoning the Estates-General, the French equivalent of Britain's Parliament.

The last time the Estates-General had met was in 1614! No elections had been held for almost 200 years. There was no one alive who remembered how the Estates-General had organized its business or voted on its decisions. So there was plenty of room for argument as well as confusion.

And there were plenty of suggestions about what the Estates-General should do, as literally hundreds of pamphlets poured from the nation's printing presses, urging virtually every kind of reform imaginable.

Many French people published pamphlets urging reforms.

11

Poor harvests in 1787 and 1788 meant that many peasants could not afford even simple food like bread.

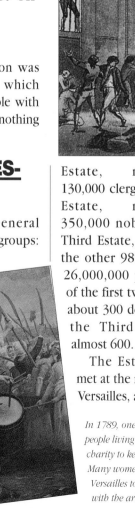

In 1787 there was a bad harvest in France - then another one in 1788. For the poor people this spelled disaster. They spent half their income on bread. High bread prices left them with almost nothing to spend on anything else. This affected makers of cloth, shoes, candles and other household goods. People fell behind with their taxes - and the government was forced to borrow. By 1788 half of all the government's income was being used to pay interest on borrowed money.

Starving peasants rioted and troops had to be called in to restore order.

In April 1789 a demonstration against an unpopular employer in Paris turned into a general riot. The riot was put down by troops, leaving 25 dead. Paris looked ready to explode into violence. Its population of over 650,000 made it five times bigger than the next largest French city. At least one in five of that huge population was living on charity - which meant 100,000 people with too little to eat and nothing to do.

THE ESTATES-GENERAL

The Estates-General consisted of three groups: the First Estate, representing 130,000 clergy; the Second Estate, representing 350,000 nobles; and the Third Estate, representing the other 98% of France's 26,000,000 people! Each of the first two estates had about 300 deputies, while the Third Estate had almost 600.

The Estates-General met at the royal palace of Versailles, about 20 miles (32 km) outside Paris, on May 5, 1789. Many of the deputies were determined not only to sort out the nation's finances, but to take the chance to bring in many other reforms as well. They saw for themselves, most for the first time, the luxury in which their ruler and his courtiers lived.

DISAGREEMENT ABOUT VOTING

From the start there was disagreement about voting. Should a decision be reached by voting as estates - or as individuals?

In 1789, one in every five people living in Paris relied on charity to keep them alive. Many women marched to Versailles to demand equality with the aristocrats.

CRASH

The king's soldiers protected the Royal Court. They were well armed and well trained.

THE NATIONAL ASSEMBLY

On June 20, the deputies of the Third Estate gathered at their usual meeting place to find that, on the king's orders, they had been locked out. So they took over a nearby indoor tennis court and swore an oath to go on meeting until they had drawn up a new constitution. One hundred and fifty of the clergy and some of the nobles also joined them.

SUMMONED BEFORE THE KING

On June 23, deputies of all three estates were summoned to hear a speech from the monarch himself. He welcomed their support in the work of reform but said he would do what he thought best anyway, whether they supported him or not. The Third Estate responded by passing a decree that any attempt to arrest any of its members would be treated as a crime punishable by death. Over the next three days, dozens more clergy and noblemen joined the National Assembly. Meanwhile, the king sent regiments of troops to stand guard over the road between Paris and Versailles.

On Saturday, July 11, Louis XVI suddenly dismissed his finance minister, Jacques Necker. Many members of the National Assembly had hoped that this clever banker might be able to get France out of its financial mess. *On Sunday it was rumored in Paris that royal troops were on the march.*

If votes were cast by the estates the clergy and nobles could protect their privileges by outvoting the Third Estate, two to one. If votes were cast by each individual deputy then the Third Estate had only to win over a few votes from either of the other estates to have a majority. Not surprisingly the clergy and nobles declared in favor of voting by estate. In reply, the Third Estate voted on June 17 to call itself the "National Assembly" and invited members of the other two estates to join it in drawing up a new constitution that would completely change the way France was governed.

This wasn't at all what the king and his ministers had in mind! Louis was quite willing to discuss his subjects' worries and problems. But he was certainly not going to hand over his right to govern the country.

On finding themselves locked out of their meeting place, the Third Estate took over a tennis court and swore to draw up a new constitution.

DID THE KING SEND TROOPS TO PARIS?

Why had the king stationed troops between Versailles and Paris? Was he worried that the National Assembly might go to Versailles? Or that it might call on the Paris mob for help against him? The king had some troops in Paris itself, including units of foreign mercenaries. But the local city militia, the French Guard, was recruited from the citizens of Paris. A move to send in large numbers of royal reinforcements might start a riot like the one that had happened in April. Would the French Guard support foreign mercenaries against fellow Parisians – or fight them?

Would the king's army fight against their fellow Frenchmen in the streets of Paris?

COULD THE NATIONAL ASSEMBLY RESIST THE KING?

Local Parisian poor people called on each other to support their new constitution, not the king.

WHAT HAPPENED NEXT?

If the king sent soldiers to disperse the National Assembly by force, the unarmed deputies could scarcely hope to fight them. But if the deputies knew in time that troops were being sent against them they could flee – either to Paris or to a city in the provinces. But if the Assembly was broken up, wouldn't its members just go home? Surely they would realize that the king had soldiers stationed throughout the nation and could simply order them to break up an Assembly wherever it met – unless it met abroad.

The king had agreed to set up the National Assembly. But would he continue to support it when he disagreed with what they said?

14

DID THE KING ORDER ANY ARRESTS?

The King might have hoped that the arrests of even a few of the National Assembly's members would frighten the rest into obedience. Or, rather than frighten them, why not just get rid of them at gunpoint? He could always hold another election and use his power over judges, mayors and other royal officials to see that no troublemakers were chosen as deputies. He could also change the rules to make sure that the nobles and clergy could outvote the Third Estate. Or he could just go ahead and order whatever reforms he thought necessary.

Louis XVI was determined to govern the country as he saw fit.

Would he try to arrest members of the National Assembly? Why had the National Assembly passed a decree declaring its members free from arrest?

CAN YOU DECIDE WHAT THE KING WILL DO NEXT?

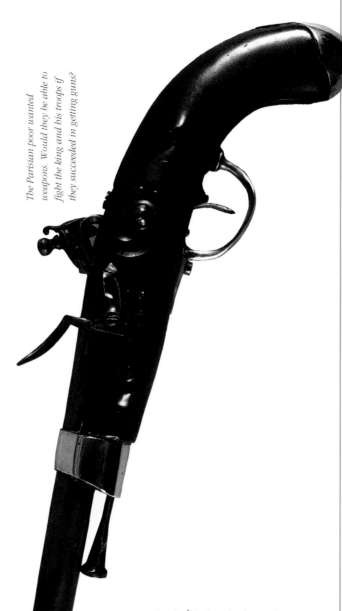

The Parisian poor wanted weapons. Would they be able to fight the king and his troops if they succeeded in getting guns?

WHAT IF FIGHTING BROKE OUT?

Some people were determined to change the government of France. They believed that if the king crushed the National Assembly their chance of reform would be gone for good. But if they could force the king to use soldiers against civilians it would show him up as a bloody tyrant. And surely the French Guard wouldn't just stand aside and see Parisians shot down? With armed troops on both sides, any fighting would be serious — and might lead to an outright revolution.

WHAT REALLY HAPPENED IN THE FRENCH REVOLUTION?

When news reached Paris on Sunday, July 12, that royal forces were on the march, a mob crowded the streets shouting support for the Third Estate. Gun shops were plundered for weapons and the French Guard militia declared its support for the Parisian people. Royal troops fled from the capital. Looting broke out.

The Bastille had become a symbol of the hated royal power. On July 14 ,1789, Parisians forced the governor of the Bastille to surrender and took over the prison.

THAT WEEK

On July 13, a new city government took charge of Paris. Its members were mostly people who had helped to choose deputies for the Estates-General. They gave orders to raise a Town Guard, but the supply of guns soon ran out. Patrols were sent onto the streets and order was restored.

On Tuesday, July 14, there were rumors that royal troops were returning to the attack. Barricades were put up, but the only soldiers to return were deserters from the royal army. Meanwhile, the search went on for more guns and gunpowder. The townspeople hesitated to attack the fortress and prison known as the Bastille.

It had a garrison of only 130, but its walls were formidable. However, after a three-hour full-scale assault with artillery the Bastille surrendered. The governor of the Bastille, de Launey, and seven of his men were murdered by the mob. The Bastille, a hated symbol of royal power, was later demolished.

The king was told that he could not rely on the obedience of his own troops. On July 15, he went to the National Assembly and agreed to withdraw his troops from Paris and to restore Necker to office. On July 17, he visited Paris and agreed that the Marquis de Lafayette, hero of the American Revolution, should command the new Town Guard. Leading nobles began to flee abroad.

AFTERWARD

Over the course of the summer there were peasant riots and attacks on the nobility throughout France. Then, in October, rumors of a royal attempt to crush the revolution led a Parisian mob to march on Versailles. The royal family was rescued by Lafayette but forced to live in Paris. A new constitution limited the king's power. Church lands were taken away to solve the country's financial problems. In June 1791 the royal family tried to flee the country but was caught and brought back.

The revolutionary government of France became more and more extreme. Thousands of former aristocrats were beheaded by the guillotine, and Louis XVI himself was executed in 1793. After many changes of government, power was seized by the Corsican Napoleon Bonaparte, who crowned himself emperor of France.

The new National Convention declared France a republic and executed the king.

WILL THIS BE THE GREATEST TRIUMPH?

Emperor Napoleon has announced his intention to invade Russia. He is the master of western Europe. Of his enemies only Spain and Britain remain defiant. Will he now conquer the East as well?

SOLDIER OF FORTUNE

Napoleon began as a soldier. Now he is a general and an emperor - a maker of laws and kings. On every field of battle he inspires the devotion of his men and the respect of his enemies. He has been winning battles now for almost 20 years. Speed and surprise have always been the keys to his greatest victories.

In 1800 Napoleon led his army through the Alps before the snow had even melted, and at Marengo he smashed an Austrian army, even though his soldiers were outnumbered. In 1805 Napoleon was forced to abandon his plans to invade Britain after his defeat by the British navy at the Battle of Trafalgar. But that same year

Napoleon declared himself Emperor in 1804.

Napoleon destroyed a combined army of Austrian and Russian troops, which once again outnumbered his own forces. The Austrians and Russians lost 26,000 men, the French 9,000.

NAPOLEON THE VICTOR

In 1806 Emperor Napoleon conquered Prussia in just six weeks with the loss of 8,000 men. The Prussians lost 11,000 dead or wounded and almost 15,000 taken as prisoners of war. Then in 1807, at Friedland, Napoleon went on to defeat a Russian army.

In 1809 Napoleon led a surprise night crossing of the River Danube to launch the greatest artillery barrage yet seen in the history of warfare - and to win another great victory over the Austrians, at Wagram.

Napoleon was a military genius, capable of defeating armies much larger than his own. Although his empire was smaller than Russia's, he still planned to invade.

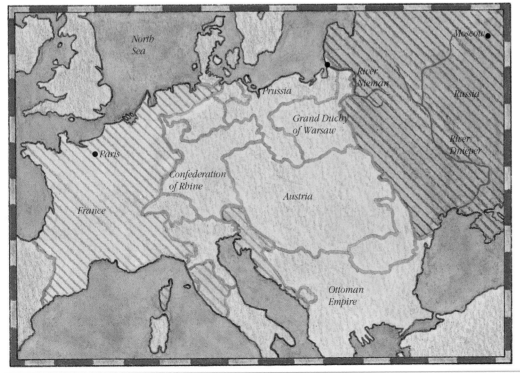

Alexander I presented the Kalmouk Cossacks and Basquirs of the Russian army to Napoleon in 1807.

I n 1807 Napoleon, emperor of France, and Alexander I, tsar of Russia, met at Tilsit. Their meeting took place on a raft in the middle of the Neman River, which marked the boundary between the territories they controlled. They signed a peace treaty – and forced Prussia to hand over much of Poland to French control. They also forced the Prussians to pay back Napoleon the money it cost him to defeat them!

NAPOLEON AND THE TSAR

Napoleon insisted that he had always wanted only peace with the tsar. But the tsar, despite the promises he had made, had never sent troops to help France against the tsar's former allies, the Austrians.

The tsar had also refused to support Napoleon's plan to starve Britain into submission by cutting off trade. Russia continued to trade with Britain. It was also well-known that many of the tsar's advisers were bitterly opposed to a French alliance. Alexander's own mother had called Napoleon a "blood-stained tyrant."

Could Napoleon leave so powerful a ruler free to defy him while Britain was still undefeated and his armies in Spain were on the verge of defeat?

In 1811 the French ambassador to Russia, General Armand de Caulaincourt, dared to contradict Napoleon when the emperor said that the tsar was afraid of him. The ambassador pointed out that Russia is an immense country. The tsar could afford to let an invader conquer vast areas, because the more an invader conquered the further he would be from the home base that sent him his supplies and provided reinforcements. Unless he was well prepared to occupy conquered areas through-out the harsh Russian winter, any invader would have to retreat, which would mean fighting off not only the Russians but the winter weather as well. Furthermore, the tsar had said that he would

Napoleon was an outstanding and courageous leader, fighting in battles such as Austerlitz.

Tsar Alexander I of Russia signed a peace treaty with Napoleon at Tilsit in 1807.

DOR'S WARNING

never sign a peace treaty, even if his army was beaten, and had warned that, "It will not be a one-day war."

INVASION!

Ignoring the ambassador's words, on June 24, 1812, Napoleon led his Grande Armée (Great Army) across the Neman River into Russian-held territory. It was the largest army ever assembled in the history of the world - 435,000 men. With reinforcements it would come to 600,000. Of these only half were French. Defeated Austria

Napoleon left food supplies along his invasion route to feed his troops.

contributed 30,000 soldiers and Prussia 20,000. The rest were from nations supposedly "liberated" by Napoleon – Poland, Italy, Germany, Holland, and Switzerland.

Napoleon foresaw that thinly populated Russia

would not provide enough food for his men to live off the land. So he made careful plans to set up a chain of supply dumps along his army's line of march. What he did not foresee was that the Russians would burn everything as they retreated before him. Nor did he expect the unusual weather that plagued his soldiers and horses - a wicked combination of scorching summer heat and driving rainstorms.

It took Napoleon three months to lead his advance guard 600 miles (900km) into Russia. The rest of his army was strung out along the entire line of march.

On September 7, at Borodino, 70 miles (112 km) west of Moscow, the Russians finally decided to make the invaders stand and fight. The sides were roughly even - about 120,000 men each. The

battle lasted 15 hours. Napoleon lost 28,000 men, the Russians 40,000. The Russian forces retreated yet again. ***Would Napoleon defeat the Russians and capture Moscow?***

Napoleon was much admired by his troops. They willingly followed him into battle during the campaigns.

Russia is a huge country and it took Napoleon three months to cover 600 miles (900 km) with his advance guard. The rest of his army was strung out along the route.

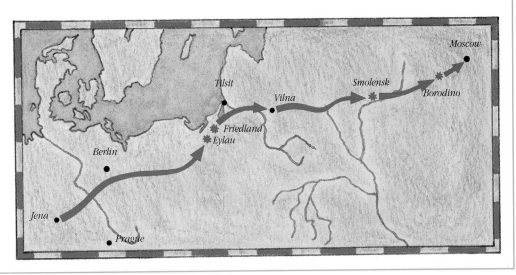

Would the Russian commander, Prince Kutuzov, gather his troops together and fight another battle before the bitterly cold winter began?

NAPOLEON BONAPARTE

WHAT HAPPENED NEXT?

DID THE RUSSIANS DEFEND MOSCOW?

The Battle of Borodino was fought to keep the French out [of] Moscow. At their current rate of march it would take the Fren[ch] another week to get to the city. There was time to prepare [the] defenses, which already included fortifications running for 25 miles (... km) around the city. Would the Grande Armée be strong enough [to] take Moscow or surround it for a siege? If the city was besieged, wh[o] would survive a winter better – the defenders, snug under cover, or t[he] besiegers in their tents? And, if the civilian population could b[e] evacuated in the week before the invaders arrived, surely a defendin[g] force could make their supplies last much longer.

them together and risk another head-on fight with Napoleon before winter set in? Or would it be wiser to keep his troops scattered, free to attack the invader's supply lines and able to find food more easily than if they were all concentrated in one place?

Did the French troops loot Moscow?

DID NAPOLEON ORDER HIS TROOPS TO LOOT THE CITY?

If Napoleon occupied the city and the tsar still refused to make peace, he could always loot the city and burn it down. The loot would enable him to reward his men for all their sufferings – and the smoking ruins of a great city would be a warning of the price for defying him.

DID THE RUSSIANS TRY TO FIGHT ANOTHER BATTLE?

The Russian commander, Kutuzov, had been beaten by Napoleon at Austerlitz and again at Borodino. But he had only sent half of his army into battle and could still call on 100,000 more men. Should he collect

Napoleon was a long way from his empire. Would he survive a winter in Moscow?

Napoleon had forced the Russians back yet again.

But he had lost a quarter of his advance guard. Winter was only two months away. How could he supply his men and keep them warm in temperatures of –22°F (–30°C)?

HOW WOULD NAPOLEON PROTECT HIS ARMY?

Napoleon's tent was warm and snug, but what about those of his troops? Would they survive the cold winter?

DID NAPOLEON OCCUPY MOSCOW?

Napoleon had built his career on victories. All his power and glory depended on continuing success. If the tsar of Russia was defeated 20 times, he was still the tsar. But if Napoleon was beaten, what was he but a failed general? He had lost individual battles, but he had never lost a campaign. He had always been able to return to Paris in triumph. If he occupied Moscow, the second city of the Russian Empire, surely the tsar would be forced to make peace to get it back? Or would Napoleon find himself trapped there with his army, cut off from the rest of his empire for the entire winter?

WHAT REALLY HAPPENED TO NAPOLEON?

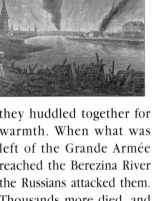

It's believed that most of the fires that destroyed Moscow were started by the retreating Russians.

The advance guard of the Grande Armée - 90,000 strong - entered Moscow a week after the Battle of Borodino only to find that the Russian governor had evacuated the city. More than 80% of the people had left. Those remaining were mostly beggars and criminals released from prison. No one came to surrender the city to Napoleon. The tsar refused even to consider the possibility of a peace treaty.

Fires had broken out and when the invaders looked for fire-fighting equipment they found that all hoses and pumps had been taken by the Russians. The fire went on for five days. Three quarters of Moscow was burned to the ground. This made it impossible to use the city as a winter headquarters while waiting for reinforcements and supplies.

Napoleon's troops marched back to the West.

AFTERWARD

On October 19, just over one month after occupying Moscow, the Grande Armée abandoned it. Weighed down with loot, the soldiers left with 150,000 horses and 40,000 wagons and barrows. Rumors started in Paris that Napoleon had died in Russia.

At first the retreating Grande Armée tried to go south, but, too weak and disorganized to risk a pitched battle, it was forced to turn back along its original route, where almost all the food supplies had been eaten during the advance. On November 9 the first French troops reached Smolensk, which they themselves had burned down less than three months before. They ate supplies intended to last for two weeks in only three days, leaving nothing for those who came after them.

DYING OF TYPHUS

On November 14 the temperature fell to 3°F (-16°C). Typhus, a highly infectious disease carried by fleas, broke out and spread quickly among the troops as they huddled together for warmth. When what was left of the Grande Armée reached the Berezina River the Russians attacked them. Thousands more died, and Napoleon himself was almost captured. By the time it left Russian territory, on December 14, the Grande Armée had been reduced to 10,000 effective troops.

BEGINNING OF THE END?

His disastrous invasion of Russia did not lead to Napoleon's immediate downfall. But it was the first campaign he had clearly lost - and the beginning of his end.

The French troops had won a battle at Smolensk, but found few supplies left there on their return.

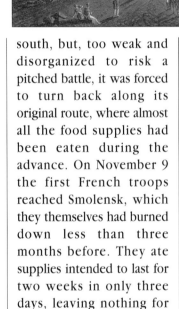

A BREAKTHROUGH FOR PEACE

The archduke Franz-Ferdinand has announced that he will go ahead with his planned visit to Sarajevo, capital of Bosnia-Herzegovina, despite fears for his personal safety. As the heir to the throne of Austria-Hungary he feels that a royal visit to this remote and troubled province will strengthen the loyalty of the local population and boost the morale of local troops and officials.

The archduke's children had no right to the throne as his parents disapproved of the marriage.

BALKAN BACKGROUND

The political situation in the Balkans is complicated and unstable.

For five centuries this Christian region has been dominated by the Muslim Ottoman Turks. Over that period, the Catholic Habsburg emperors of Austria have gradually pushed their borders south, liberating Hungary from Ottoman rule and adding it to their lands. Although Bosnia-Herzegovina was occupied by Austrian troops in 1878 it became a formal part of the Austro-Hungarian Empire only in 1908. A new constitution tries to ensure that each of the three groups that make up its population - Orthodox Christians, Roman Catholics, and Muslims - has a say in government.

THE RECENT WARS

Between two empires - the Austro-Hungarian Empire to the north and the Ottoman to the south - lies a belt of mountainous territory controlled by new states that are fiercely proud of their independence. In 1912 an alliance of these Balkan states - Bulgaria, Greece, Montenegro, and Serbia - drove the Ottoman army out of most of the remaining territories it controlled in Europe. A peace conference held in London in May 1913 divided these territories between the victors and created a new state, Albania. A month later Bulgaria, unhappy about its share, attacked Greece and Serbia, but was beaten back.

As a result of these wars Serbia has doubled in size. However, it now looks westward to neighboring Bosnia-Herzegovina, where fellow Orthodox Christians live under the rule of Catholic Austria, and even Muslims have the same rights as Serbs.

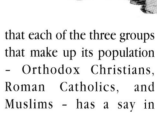

The Balkan states cover much of southeastern Europe. They have had a turbulent history.

WHY ARE THEY

Secret societies are supposed to be secret, but the Black Hand is a very open secret. It was formed in the Serbian capital, Belgrade, in 1911. Its aim is to unite all Serbians living under foreign rule with the people of independent Serbia. Its motto is "Unity or Death." Its members are mostly young officers or students. Its methods are clearly suggested by its seal, which incorporates a skull and crossbones, a bomb, a dagger, and a vial of poison. Its leader is known as Colonel Apis, but he is almost certainly Dragutin Dimitrijevic, the head of Serbian military intelligence.

WHY ARE THEY GOING?

What is this royal visit supposed to achieve?

Archduke Franz-Ferdinand, as inspector general of the Austro-Hungarian armed forces, is to watch military maneu-

vers in the mountains near Sarajevo. His presence is intended to reassure the officers and men serving in this troublesome area that their efforts are being appreciated in Vienna. It should also serve notice to the Serbs that Austria is on the alert and ready to defend its frontiers against any attack.

PEACEFUL MISSION

Meanwhile the archduke's wife, Duchess Sophie of Hohenburg, is scheduled to visit both schools and orphanages in the Bosnian capital.

The archduke wanted his visit to be of cultural as well as military importance. He took time to meet some of the religious leaders in Sarajevo.

In archduke Franz-Ferdinand's eyes, his wife's role in the Sarajevo visit may be just as important as his own. It is well-known that their marriage was opposed by the royal household because the future duchess was only the daughter of a poor Czech nobleman. Before he was allowed to marry her, the archduke had to agree that she would not become a full member of the Habsburg family and that none of their children would inherit the throne. She is required to walk behind him in processions and may not sit next to him at any state banquets or other formal events in Austria-Hungary.

The archduke deeply

GOING TO SARAJEVO?

On foreign visits, such as a trip to Sarajevo, Duchess Sophie was allowed to walk beside her husband. Local dignitaries greeted the couple and treated them both as royalty.

resents these insults and welcomes the opportunity that this visit gives for his wife to be treated with respect by the people. The date planned for their visit is their 14th wedding anniversary.

AND WHAT OF THE DANGERS?

The archduke is a brave man and has survived three assassination attempts already. "One has to rely upon God," is known to be his motto.

COUNTDOWN

The royal couple arrived in Sarajevo by train at about 9:45 in the morning of Sunday, June 28, 1914. The military governor of the province, General Potiorek, was there to welcome them. A fleet of six cars stood by to take the visitors to a reception in the town hall, where they would meet local officials and leaders of the different local communities. The archduke and duchess, both splendidly dressed, sat in an open-topped car so that they could be seen by and wave to the crowds that had turned out in large numbers to line the streets.

The route to the reception passed along Appel Quay, a long, narrow street, with the Milijacka River on one side and rows of closely packed shops and houses on the other. In the event of a riot or an assassination attempt it would be very difficult for the driver of the arch-duke's car to do anything but keep on going forward – provided that the road wasn't blocked. The road was too narrow for the car to turn around, and reversing would mean backing up the whole motorcade.

PEACEFUL VISIT

To emphasize the happy nature of the royal visit it had been decided that there should be no soldiers lining the streets. The Austrian authorities did not like to admit that its troops were, in effect, an army of occupation and preferred to give the impression that the local people were entirely happy to be under their rule.

THE BLACK HAND

All was going smoothly until the motorcade arrived at Cumurija Bridge, just after ten o'clock. *Then Nedelijko Cabrinovic, a member of the Black Hand, stepped forward from the crowd lining the street and threw a bomb toward the car that was carrying the royal couple....*

Nedelijko Cabrinovic had no problems getting close to the archduke's car as there were no soldiers in the streets.

The police would be watching anyone who tried to get close to the archduke, but would they save him?

WOULD THE ASSASSINS BE CAUGHT?

The best guarantee for the success of an assassination is for the killer to get as close as possible to the victim. Unfortunately for the assassin, this greatly increases the likelihood of being captured. Suppose a first assassination failed and the assassin (or assassins) escaped in the confusion – would he try again? An assassin is usually well aware of the risks involved. If he was not killed on the spot, he might be executed later. Capture might also result in torture, in order to find out which organization – or government – was behind the deed.

DID THEY CARRY ON WITH THEIR VISIT?

Suppose the bomb failed to detonate, or that it exploded but failed to injure the royal party. Would the visit continue? The archduke was known to believe that he simply had to get on with his duty as a soldier and future leader of his people, whatever the risks. He might also take the view that lightning wouldn't strike twice in the same place on the same day. So, presuming that he was not injured, he would certainly have wanted to deny the terrorists a propaganda victory. How would it look if the heir to the throne went scuttling back to Vienna

Vienna. The old city's narrow streets and the large crowds of onlookers would make it far harder to protect a target – especially one who had purposely come to show himself off to the public.

The Black Hand was not short of young volunteers who would sacrifice their lives for the cause. If the first attempt to assassinate the archduke failed, there were many others eager to make a second attempt.

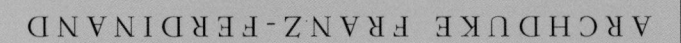

WHAT HAPPENED NEXT?

ARCHDUKE FRANZ-FERDINAND

A pistol at close range would give an assassin the best chance of success, but would he be able to get away afterward?

The archduke and duchess wanted their visit to be as friendly as possible, so they used an open-topped car, despite its lack of security.

after a botched attempt on his life? What would the effect be on the morale of his troops, who were risking their lives to defend their country's frontiers? On the other hand, would the archduke risk the life of the duchess? And would General Potiorek, who was responsible for the safety of the heir to the throne, allow the visit to continue? He had failed to prevent one assassination attempt, so he could no longer guarantee the archduke's safety.

WHO WOULD GET THE BLAME?

In the event of a successful assassination, who would get the blame? General Potiorek would presumably be held responsible for the failure of security. But the net would spread wider. Would the local Serb population in Sarajevo be made to suffer for harboring the killer? Would the Serbian government itself be blamed? If it were, would this lead to war?

The archduke and his wife were risking their lives by visiting Sarajevo

Were they injured by the bomb? Would there be another attempt to kill them? What would happen if they did die?

CAN YOU DECIDE WHAT HAPPENED IN THAT NARROW STREET IN SARAJEVO?

WOULD THERE BE A SECOND ATTEMPT TO KILL THEM?

Anyone wanting to assassinate a high-ranking Austrian would know that the archduke's visit to Sarajevo would be the best opportunity they were ever likely to get. In Vienna security would be much tighter and secret police surveillance much more effective. Among Sarajevo's mixed population a Serb stranger would attract much less notice than in faraway

A flag symbolizes unity, and the Serbian flag united all the people of Serbia. Would they all be blamed if the archduke was killed?

WHAT REALLY HAPPENED TO THE ARCHDUKE?

Cabrinovic's bomb bounced off the back of the archduke's car and exploded under the following vehicle, wounding two officers and about 20 onlookers. The archduke stopped his own car, checked that the wounded were being cared for, then sped on to the town hall.

Gavrilo Princip succeeded in assassinating the archduke.

The enraged archduke cut short the reception at the town hall to visit his injured aides in a nearby military hospital. The duchess insisted on going with him. But the drivers at the front of the motorcade thought that the visit was continuing as previously planned and, at the appropriate turning, swung off toward the cathedral. As the driver of the archduke's car started to turn back,

Gavrilo Princip stepped forward with a raised pistol.

A policeman tried to tackle Princip, but he was stopped by another Black Hand member. Princip had time to go to within a few paces of the car and fire several times before the police overpowered him. The archduke was hit in the neck, the duchess in the stomach. Doctors could save neither of them.

AFTERWARD

Five out of six of the Black Hand assassins were caught. None of the assassins was over 20 years old. On account of their youth Cabrinovic and Princip were spared the death penalty, and both were sentenced to 20 years' hard labor.

In the streets of Vienna, students staged anti-Serb demonstrations. In Belgrade, on the other hand, Serbian newspapers made no secret of their satisfaction at the assassination and the government did noth-ing to investigate whether the Black Hand was involved.

Austria saw that the assassination provided an excuse for war with Serbia. On July 23 it sent a ten-point ultimatum to Serbia. The Serbs agreed to almost everything but refused to allow Austrian officials to take part in a joint inquiry into the archduke's

The archduke was fatally wounded by a pistol shot. This is an artist's impression of how it looked.

assassination.

On July 28 the Austro-Hungarian army prepared for war. The next day Russia, Austria's rival for control of the Balkans and self-appointed guardian of fellow Orthodox Serbs, also mobilized for war. Germany, Austria's ally, called upon Russia to stop and asked France, Russia's ally, to stay neutral if war broke out between Germany and Russia. When its requests were ignored, Germany declared war on Russia and invaded Luxembourg so that it could use its railroads to take over Belgium. This was part of the German plan to knock France out before it could aid Russia. But by violating the neutrality of Belgium, Germany ensured that Britain would step in to fight alongside France and Russia. World War I had begun.

World War I was "the war to end all wars." At least 20 million people were killed before it ended.

WHO FIRED THE GUNS?

Tsar Nicholas II was well respected and loved by the Russian people.

There is yet another new crisis in Russia. After three years of military disasters, and with the government in complete chaos, St. Petersburg, the capital itself now appears to be under bombardment! Could it be a revolution?

"LITTLE FATHER"

For centuries, Russia has expanded its territories eastward to become the largest country in the world. Its ruler, the tsar, lives in splendor in the stunning and beautiful capital of St. Petersburg, re-named Petrograd in 1914. But 90% of the Russian people are peasants, who live in great poverty. They must pay heavy taxes and send their sons to serve in the army without pay. Fewer than one in five of the population can read or even write.

The Duma, the national parliament, is a new institution and is weak and divided. Until a few months ago all important decisions were made by Tsar Nicholas II and his officials. But despite all their suffering, the poor, ordinary Russian people are still devoted to their "Little Father," the Tsar.

ENEMIES WITHIN

For more than a century, Russian governments have been using spies, informers, and secret police to hunt down conspirators and revolutionaries who have tried to change the system by force. In 1861, Tsar Alexander II freed the peasants from serfdom and gave them the right to buy the land they worked. But his government remained severe in putting down any unrest and, after two unsuccessful attempts on his life, assassins finally succeeded in killing him with a bomb in 1881.

The Russian government has tried to improve living and working conditions, but many different kinds of agitators are still active among the workers. Socialists want to end the great gap in wealth between the rich and the poor. Communists want to create a government of soviets, meaning councils chosen by ordinary people, which they say will make everyone equal.

The royal family was extremely wealthy, owning many beautiful jewels, such as this diamond spray.

Most Russians were poor peasants who lived in isolated villages. Few could read or write.

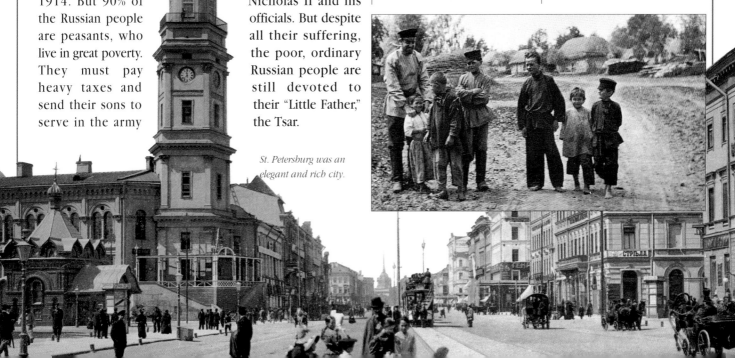

St. Petersburg was an elegant and rich city.

DEFEAT

Would Stolypin be able to steer the country away from revolution?

There had already been one full-scale attempt at revolution in Russia. In February 1904 war broke out between Russia and Japan over control of Korea and Manchuria. Although Russia had a much larger army than Japan, it could not make full use of its troops because the war was being fought so far away. Russian forces had to be supplied by means of the Trans-Siberian Railway over a distance of 5,000 miles (8,000 km). To everyone's surprise, Russia found itself losing the war. On January 1, 1905, the Russians surrendered their besieged base at Port Arthur to the Japanese.

BLOODY SUNDAY

Back in St. Petersburg workers went on strike to protest about their harsh lives and to demand change. On January 2, a huge, peaceful crowd of 200,000 demonstrators marched to the Winter Palace to present a petition to the tsar begging him for reforms to end their misery. But before they got to the palace they were met by troops, who opened fire without warning, killing over 500 unarmed people.

This "Bloody Sunday" led to more than a year of rampant riots, strikes, and assassinations, which spread right across Russia. In June 1905 the crew of the battleship *Potemkin* mutinied. In October Tsar Nicholas II promised that the country should have a Duma (parliament) for the first time and be governed by a new constitution. In December there was a bloody uprising in the streets of Moscow, Russia's second city. By the time the riots and strikes had been put down, 15,000 people had been killed and 70,000 arrested. A Duma was called but then dismissed after it passed a vote of no confidence in the tsar's ministers. There was no new constitution.

REFORM AND RECOVERY

In 1906, Nicholas II appointed a clever and hardworking man, Pyotr Arkadyevich Stolypin, as his prime minister. Stolypin introduced reforms that gave the peasants more control over the land they worked. Peasants were also allowed to run for election to local councils and to get jobs as government officials too. Stolypin was assassinated in 1911. But things still seemed to be getting better.

Then, in 1914, Russia got drawn into World War I.

The Russian army was twice as big as the German or French army, but it was badly equipped and poorly trained. Soldiers were sometimes sent into battle without rifles. In the first months of fighting the Russian army lost about 200,000 men as killed, wounded, or captured. The final figure for Russian

The poor Russian peasants fought in the streets of St. Petersburg .

men dead, wounded, and captured was at least five million.

Short of food and ammunition, and with transport and medical aid in chaos, the Russian soldiers still went on fighting. Meanwhile the tsar's government was so divided by squabbling that in less than 12 months there were four different prime ministers, three different war ministers, and three different foreign ministers. The tsar called a Duma to get support for the war effort, then

AND REVOLT

The new war minister, Alexander Kerensky, was determined to carry on the war effort.

dismissed it for a while, then called it back again.

THE FEBRUARY REVOLUTION

The breaking point came in the spring of 1917. What happened has become known as the "February Revolution" because Russia still followed the Julian calendar, which is 11 days "behind" the Gregorian calendar used by Western countries (the dates used here are Western style).

On March 8 demonstrations broke out in Petrograd (St. Petersburg). Two days later, the soldiers refused to fire on demonstrators and joined them instead. The Duma decided to replace the government of the tsar with a provisional government chosen from its own members. But at the same time a determined group of revolutionaries, the Bolsheviks, set up a rival government called the Soviet of Workers' and Soldiers' Deputies. (The word *soviet* means "council.")On March 15, Tsar Nicholas II gave up the throne in favor of his

Lenin was a dedicated revolutionary but he had spent many years in exile. Did he still understand Russia?

brother, Grand Duke Michael, who held power for one day before turning the reins of government over to the Provisional Government.

THE STRUGGLE FOR POWER

There were now two rival governments calling on the people to obey them. Both promised reforms, but both said it was vital to win the war first.

On April 16 a middle-aged, bearded man came home to Russia after ten years exile in Switzerland. His name was Vladimir Ilyich Ulyanov, but he was better known as Lenin. He became the most dedicated and ruthless of the Bolshevik leaders and soon took over their organization and began to use the Soviet to stir up trouble for the Provisional Government. Lenin saw how weary the Russian people were of war and put his program for them into just three words: "peace, bread, land."

Despite the opposition of the Soviet, the Provisional Government launched new offensives against the Germans in June and July, directed by an inspiring new war minister, Alexander Kerensky. The first

offensive failed after a week when soldiers refused to obey orders. The second was pushed back by the enemy after some early successes.

Lenin thought that these failures gave him a good chance to overthrow the Provisional Government and on July 16 the Bolsheviks organized demonstrations by sailors and their own Red Guards. But these were put down by troops loyal to the Provisional Government. On July 18 Lenin fled over the border to Finland. On July 20 Kerensky became prime minister.

For the moment it looked as though the Provisional Government had won the struggle for power. But Kerensky quarreled with his commander in chief, General Kornilov, who wanted to crush the remaining Bolsheviks by force. Meanwhile the

Germans continued to advance and took the Baltic port of Riga, less than 400 miles (about 600 km) from Petrograd. When Kornilov tried to seize power for himself in September, Kerensky appealed to the Bolsheviks for their support and had Kornilov and his fellow generals arrested. Meanwhile, Lenin quietly slipped back from hiding in Finland.

On the evening of October 25 the guns of the cruiser **Aurora,** *at anchor in the Neva River, suddenly boomed out over the Russian capital....*

Modern warships such as the Aurora *had immensely destructive firepower.*

WOULD A STRUGGLE FOR POWER LEAD TO RUSSIA'S DEFEAT IN WAR?

The firing of the guns of the *Aurora* could scarcely be kept a secret. Even if the Germans didn't have spies in the capital, they would surely learn about any sort of street fighting between armed groups. This would certainly encourage the Germans to carry on with their invasion until they had taken the capital itself and forced whatever government was left in Russia to accept peace on their terms.

The breakdown of army discipline created the threat of mob rule. Would militant groups rise up from within Russia.

THE RUSSIAN REVOLUTION

WHAT HAPPENED NEXT?

DID THEY RESTORE POWER TO THE TSAR?

The tsar may have led Russia into chaos and defeat, but no one had done any better since he fell from power. There were still many Russians who would rather see their country governed by a tsar - as it had been for centuries - than by a bunch of politicians from the Duma or, worse still, a gang of revolutionaries who had spent half their lives in prison or abroad.

DID KERENSKY OR LENIN TAKE CONTROL?

Kerensky and Lenin were the two men best placed to emerge as Russia's undisputed leader. But Kerensky's summer offensives had failed, and he had survived Kornilov's challenge only by calling on the Bolsheviks. Lenin's attempt to seize power in July had failed, and he had only just returned from hiding in Finland. And both men were surrounded by ambitious followers who might try to push them aside.

The tsar's family, the Romanovs, had ruled Russia for three centuries. Did the Russian people really want this to end?

Kerensky (second from right) wanted power. Would he and his generals seize control?

WOULD THERE BE CIVIL WAR?

Whether the *Aurora* was firing to defend the capital or to destroy it, Russia had clearly reached a major crisis. If there was a moment to gamble everything on the chance of seizing power, this was it. But neither of the two main contenders could be sure of winning outright. When the Bolsheviks had tried to take control in July they had failed. And when Kerensky's Provisional Government had faced Kornilov's rebellion it was forced to call on the Bolsheviks for help. Any direct conflict between the two sides would surely lead to a long and bloody civil war before one or the other won.

WOULD LENIN OR KERENSKY SEIZE CONTROL?

Lenin had returned to Russia. But why was the *Aurora* bombarding Petrograd? *Had the Germans continued their advance eastward to the Russian capital itself? Or was the cruiser being used by another Russian general to seize power for himself?*

WHAT REALLY HAPPENED TO THE TSAR?

The Bolsheviks stormed the Winter Palace, forcing the Provisional Government to surrender.

The *Aurora* was firing blanks at Petrograd. Its volleys harmed no one, but it was the signal for the Bolsheviks to seize power by armed force. Within hours they had taken control of the railroad stations, the telephone exchange, and the central bank – with scarcely any bloodshed. On the following day, the members of the Provisional Government fled to the Winter Palace, which was bombarded until they surrendered the morning afterward.

AFTERWARD

In November, Lenin confiscated all land and property belonging to the Church and the aristocracy. Kerensky attempted to seize power from the Bolsheviks, but he failed. He escaped and spent the rest of his life in France, Australia, and the U.S. He died in 1970.

A cease-fire was arranged with the Germans in December 1917. The Bolsheviks established a new secret police force, the Cheka, to hunt down their enemies. Then, in March 1918 Russia signed the Treaty of Brest-Litovsk and gave up huge areas of its western territories.

The tsar was forced to abdicate and give up his right to rule.

However, this treaty was canceled by Germany's defeat at the hands of the Allies in November 1918.

The tsar and his family were captured by the Bolsheviks and murdered in July 1918. The following three years saw civil wars, peasant revolts, mutinies in the armed forces, and major famines that killed millions. Finally, the Bolsheviks established a Communist government that gave all power to party officials. The Communists were to rule Russia and, later, many neighboring countries until the 1980s.

The tsar and his family were held captive by the Bolsheviks until July 1918, when they were all murdered.

WILL AMERICA FIGHT?

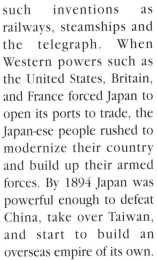

President Woodrow Wilson (left) was known as a great peacemaker.

The world is at war. Can the United States continue to stand aside? Even if they are not drawn into the war in Europe, relations with Japan seem to be at a breaking point.

RELUCTANT WARRIOR

It took three years for the United States to enter the World War I. (Repeated German attacks on neutral American shipping had pushed outraged public opinion into actively supporting the Allied side.) The United States lost some 50,000 dead – comparatively few casualties compared to the millions Britain, France, Germany, and Russia lost. But that war has made Americans anxious not to get involved in any more foreign quarrels.

The United States even refused to join the League of Nations, which was supposed to help settle international disputes peacefully. Ironically, the League was set up by the American president, Woodrow Wilson!

During the depression years of the 1930s, with nearly twelve million Americans out of work, the U.S. has been far too concerned with its own problems to want to get mixed up in Europe's arguments again. And if there is a threat to the U.S. it seems far more likely to come from quite the opposite direction.

THE RISING SUN

Less than 100 years ago, Japan was totally cut off from other countries. Its people knew nothing of such inventions as railways, steamships and the telegraph. When Western powers such as the United States, Britain, and France forced Japan to open its ports to trade, the Japan-ese people rushed to modernize their country and build up their armed forces. By 1894 Japan was powerful enough to defeat China, take over Taiwan, and start to build an overseas empire of its own.

In 1904-1905 Japan defeated Russia and took over Korea. At the Paris Peace Conference after World War I, Japan was accepted as one of the "Five Great Powers." But Japan failed to get the other powers to agree that the charter of the new League of Nations should contain a clause stating that all races were equal. The Japanese felt deeply insulted and resentful. They had struggled hard to catch up with Western countries, but felt that they were still not being accepted as equals.

In 1924 the United States made the situation worse by establishing quotas on the number of Japanese and other Asians that would be permitted to settle in this country as immigrants.

The Hawaiian Islands are situated in the Pacific Ocean.

The Great Depression of the 1930s affected both Japan and the U.S.

WHICH WAY

From the 1920s onward, Japan's leaders were divided about the country's future. Most of the civilian politicians and diplomats still wanted trade and cooperation with the Western powers to continue. But some extremists and many army officers thought Japan should build up its overseas empire, by war if necessary. Then, in 1929 and the early 1930s, world trade collapsed and Japan, like the U.S. and other Western countries, was plunged into a crisis as businesses collapsed and millions of people were thrown out of work.

Japan's "Rising Sun" flag symbolized the expansion of its overseas empire.

THE STRUGGLE FOR CHINA

In 1931 officers of the Japanese army launched an invasion of Manchuria, a huge province of north-eastern China, rich in iron and other raw materials. In 1932 they declared this region to be an independent state, Manchukuo. In fact, all real power has been kept in Japanese hands. When the League of Nations condemned the Japanese takeover, Japan left the League.

In 1937 the Japanese army went on the attack again, and invaded China itself. By the end of that year, the major cities of Peking, Nanking and Shanghai were all in Japanese hands.

On 12 December 1937 Japanese aircraft bombed and sank the American gunboat *Panay,* which was carrying Chinese refugees on the Yangtse River. Japan did not wish to provoke a war with the U.S. and apologized. A month later, President Franklin D. Roosevelt called on Congress to vote funds so that the American navy and army could be expanded.

Fighting in China continued throughout 1938 as the Japanese met fierce resistance. Western opinion was horrified by the Japanese bombing of Chinese cities and the casualties suffered by innocent civilians. Japan ignored American and

Emperor Hirohito was crowned in 1926. The Japanese thought of him as a god.

British protests that China's independence was guaranteed by a treaty that Japan itself had signed. America and Britain loaned money and sent supplies to the Chinese to support their resistance.

A WIDENING WAR

When war broke out in Europe in September 1939, President Roosevelt broadcast to the American people to assure them that the United States would remain neutral. Two months later, however, he got Congress to agree that arms could be supplied to the nations that were fighting - which enabled

FOR JAPAN?

General Tojo became prime minister of Japan in October 1941.

The Samurai sword became a symbol of Japan's military tradition.

him to send badly needed aid to Britain.

In the spring of 1940 the Germans conquered Belgium, the Netherlands, Denmark, and Norway; by summer France, too, had been defeated. It seemed as though isolated Britain might also fall.

The Japanese military saw the chance to extend their war beyond China and seize the colonies of the defeated Western powers in Southeast Asia, which were rich in rubber, tin, oil, and other vital resources.

GOING TO THE BRINK

The American government became increasingly worried at Japan's growing power and aggression. In May 1940 it ordered a major strengthening of the its fleet stationed at Pearl Harbor, on the mid-Pacific island of Hawaii. Two months later the president signed plans that would enable the Americans to have a powerful navy in both the Pacific and the Atlantic.

In September, Japanese troops began to move into French Indochina (Vietnam, Laos, and Cambodia). In the same month peacetime military service was introduced for the first time in American history. In July 1940 the U.S. banned the export of scrap iron and steel, which Japan needed for its armaments industry. On September 27, Japan announced a ten-year alliance with Germany and Italy.

In May 1941 President Roosevelt proclaimed a state of national emergency. A month later the government of occupied France announced that Japan was to have complete military control of its colonies in Indochina. In October Prince Konoye, the Japanese prime minister, who had hoped to reach a peaceful settlement of differences with the U.S., resigned and was replaced by General Tojo. Tojo announced that American and British influence in Asia would have to end.

On December 6 President Roosevelt asked the Japanese emperor, Hirohito, to intervene personally to prevent the confrontation between the two nations from leading to war. Meanwhile, in Washington, face-to-face negotiations between Japanese and American diplomats were held in a last-ditch effort to avoid conflict.

"CLIMB MOUNT NIITAKE"

On November 26, 1941, a Japanese task force consisting of six aircraft carriers, several submarines, cruisers, destroyers, other surface ships, and 432 aircraft left the Kuril Islands north of Japan and headed south. A week later, the leader of the task force and commander in chief of the Japanese navy, Admiral Yamamoto, gave the order "Climb Mount Niitake." *What did this strange order mean? Why were the Japanese heading for Pearl Harbor?...*

Naval power would prove decisive in the struggle between Japan and the U.S.

American navy personnel often relaxed on the beach over a weekend. Would the Japanese surprise them on a day of rest?

DID THE JAPANESE KNOCK OUT PEARL HARBOR?

The first wave of Japanese aircraft approached their target from 12,000 feet (3,650 m), shielded from ground observers by thick clouds. As they came down through the cloud cover around 7:40 A.M. they saw no shortage of targets - eight immense battleships and 86 other vessels, all sleeping at anchor. At the five other airfields under attack the targets were just as open -

WHAT HAPPENED NEXT?

PEARL HARBOR

DID THE JAPANESE ACHIEVE SURPRISE?

The Japanese task force was made up of more than 20 ships and had to cross over 4,000 miles (about 6,500 km) of ocean. It had been at sea for 12 days before it came within striking distance of its target. Plenty of time, one would have thought, for such a large group of vessels to be spotted - either by American air patrols or even by merchant shipping sailing accidentally across its path.

At 7:15 on the morning of Sunday, December 7, an American radar operator located a force of aircraft entering Hawaiian airspace. But the young Air Corps officer to whom he reported this was not surprised as he was expecting the arrival of a formation of American B-17 Flying Fortress aircraft.

sent from Washington to the forces in Hawaii. Despite this message no orders were given to lower steel nets to protect battleships at anchor from torpedo attack.

Hawaii had a large number of Japanese immigrants. Many were loyal American citizens, but the military were afraid that some would still fight for Japan. So, the planes at the islands' airfields, instead of being dispersed under cover, were parked close together where they could be more easily guarded from saboteurs.

If the Americans knew an attack was imminent, why did they not protect themselves?

If the Americans were anticipating an attack, why were their aircraft all exposed in the open?

WERE THE AMERICANS EXPECTING AN ATTACK?

As early as January 1941 the American ambassador in Japan, Joseph C. Grew, warned that Japan might attempt a surprise attack against Pearl Harbor. Having broken the Japanese ciphers, the U.S. knew by November 1941 that the Japanese were planning to launch a major offensive.

On November 27, 1941, a "war warning" message was

STEP IN THE CONFLICT?

CAN YOU DECIDE THE NEXT

Did Japan make a formal declaration of war? Would the attack cripple the U.S. navy? Would this strike lead to the complete Japanese conquest of Asia?

The Japanese task force was about to launch a major attack on the U.S. navy in Pearl Harbor.

---

dozens of planes parked close together out in the open.

However, if a formation of fighter planes was in the air, their tremendous firepower could inflict serious damage on a large flight of planes and, at the least, distract them into dogfights so that they could not carry out their mission.

HOW WOULD AMERICA REACT?

If the Japanese managed to cripple the American fleet, would the American public want war? Or would they prefer their country to remain neutral despite the attack. Perhaps the Americans would realize that they were facing a skilled and determined opponent - and back off? Would they also realize that war with Japan would almost inevitably mean a war with its allies, Germany and Italy, as well? Was the United States prepared to accept the challenge of a global war that would certainly last for years - and might end in defeat?

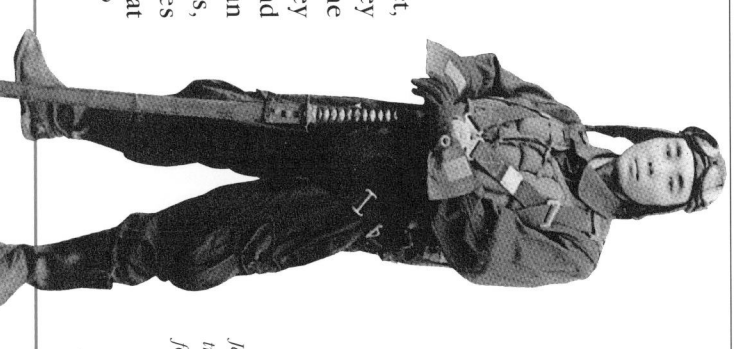

Japanese pilots were well trained and prepared to die for their cause.

WHAT REALLY HAPPENED AT PEARL HARBOR?

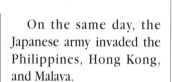

The Americans could offer very little defence against the Japanese attack.

A formal declaration of war was sent from Tokyo to the Japanese embassy in Washington on the morning of the attack. As it was a Sunday morning, however, there were only a couple of diplomats on duty. By the time they had decoded the message, typed it up and attempted to deliver it, Pearl Harbor was already being bombed.

The Japanese attack was a total surprise. Even before he dropped his first bomb the leading pilot of the first wave sent the signal for an undetected approach – "Tora! Tora! Tora!" ("Tiger! Tiger! Tiger!") Six of the giant warships anchored in Battleship Row were hit.

In less than two hours the Japanese sank or seriously damaged 18 ships, destroyed 188 planes and crippled 159 others. About 2,000 Americans died, including 68 civilians, and many more were wounded. The Japanese lost 29 planes and 55 men.

The Japanese achieved total surprise.

On the same day, the Japanese army invaded the Philippines, Hong Kong, and Malaya.

AFTERWARD

The Japanese failed to find three American aircraft carriers because they were at sea. Twenty American cruisers and 65 destroyers survived intact. The attackers also failed to demolish Pearl Harbor's oil storage tanks. Had they done so, the American Navy could not have moved against them. And had they hit the shipyards, it would have been impossible to undertake any repairs. As it was, five of the seven damaged battleships were repaired and sent back into action.

Admiral Kimmel, commander of the U.S. Pacific Fleet, and General Short, com-mander of the Army forces in Hawaii, were found guilty of "dereliction of duty" and relieved of their commands. On December 8, President Roosevelt denounced Japan's sneak attack as "a day that will live in infamy." Congress voted for war.

After the war, Admiral Chester Nimitz, American victor of the Pacific war at sea, noted that if the fleet at Pearl Harbor *had* known of the impending attack it would have sailed out to meet the Japanese task force – and would have been wiped out by better ships, manned by more-experienced crews.

The attack failed to destroy Pearl Harbor's oil storage tanks.

40

INDEX